Storytime

for

5

Year Olds

QED
QED Publishing

Copyright © QED Publishing 2011

First published in the UK in 2011 by
QED Publishing
A Quarto Group Company
226 City Road
London EC1V 2TT
www.qed-publishing.co.uk

A catalogue record for this book is available from the British Library.

ISBN 978 1 84835 622 1

Printed in China

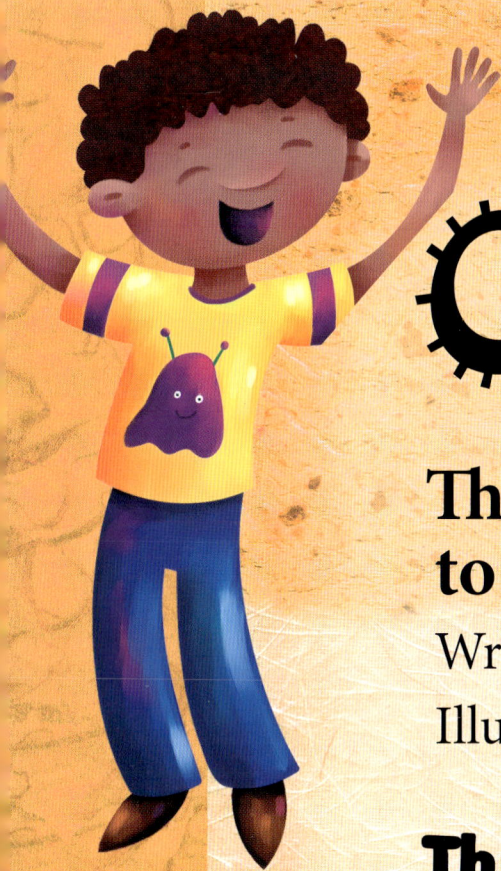

Contents

The Littlest
Lighthouse
Keeper
to the
Rescue

Henry was a very little mouse who lived in a lighthouse. He helped the lighthouse keeper with his job of guiding the ships in safely.

One night, there was a
noisy storm raging outside.
Lightning flashed and
thunder rumbled. It was
so loud that Henry
couldn't sleep.

7

When Henry woke up in the morning, he opened his porthole and looked outside.

The stormy night had turned into a lovely, sunny morning. The sky was a brilliant blue.

But what was that noise? Someone was crying.

From high up in the lighthouse, Henry couldn't see who it was.

Grabbing his cap, he scampered down the stairs to find out.

9

It didn't take Henry long to find out where the sound was coming from. Hiding under a pile of green seaweed was a tiny baby seal. Henry crept up to her.

"What's the matter?" he asked.

"I was washed up here by the storm last night," cried Baby Seal. She was very upset indeed. "I'm hungry and scared. I want to go home, but I don't know where I am."

What would Baby Seal eat?
Henry tried his own favourite foods.

Would she like
cheese?

Would she
like cake?

Would she like chocolate?

No. Baby Seal didn't like any of those things. She just cried louder.

Suddenly, a friendly voice called from the sky.
"Hi, Henry!" said the voice. It was Henry's friend, Puffin. "What's the problem?" he asked.

"Baby Seal is lost and hungry and I don't know what to do," said Henry.

Puffin smiled – he knew exactly what to do. He flew off and soon came back, holding a big fish in his beak.

Baby Seal gobbled the fish up at once.
She wasn't hungry any more. Then they all
agreed to search for Baby Seal's mother.

They set off. Puffin carried Henry on his back and Baby Seal swam along below. The sea seemed to go on forever, without any sign of Baby Seal's mother. Just when the search seemed hopeless, they saw a whale and her calf.

"Baby Seal got lost in the storm," Henry explained to the whale. "We are looking for her mother. Have you seen her?"

"No, I'm sorry, I haven't," puffed Whale. "Have you asked Albatross? He might have seen her."

They searched a little longer and soon found Albatross flying fast and high over the sea.

"I've flown hundreds of miles," said Albatross. "I've seen ships, islands and icebergs, but I haven't seen Baby Seal's mother. I'm very sorry."

"Ask Turtle if you can find him," he called. "He's usually swimming around here somewhere."

They soon found Turtle swimming nearby.
He was sad to hear about lost Baby Seal, but
didn't know where her mother was either.

"I'm sorry that I can't help," he spluttered. "I missed the storm. We were following the jellyfish from warmer seas. But I did happen to meet some dolphins who'd been in the storm. You could ask them where Baby Seal's mother is. They might be able to help."

The day was drawing to a close. Henry was fed up. They had searched for Baby Seal's mother for hours and hadn't found her anywhere. They were all very tired and Baby Seal was starting to cry again. As the sun began to set, they sat on a buoy for a rest.

Just then, a friendly dolphin popped his head above the water.

"You all look a little sad," said Dolphin. "What's wrong?"

Henry told Dolphin about lost Baby Seal. Dolphin suddenly looked very happy. "I've seen Baby Seal's mother!" he cried.

Henry, Puffin and Baby Seal followed Dolphin all the way back to the coast. There, sitting on the rocks and catching the last of the day's sunlight, were a group of seals.

"Can you see your mother? Is she there?" asked Henry. But Baby Seal couldn't see her mother anywhere. She shook her head sadly.

They moved a little closer to the seals to get a better look. "Can you see your mother now?" Henry asked. Baby Seal looked closely, but shook her head again.

Although Baby Seal didn't see her mother, her mother saw her.

She raced over to give Henry and Baby Seal a big hug. "Thank you for bringing my baby back!" cried Mother Seal. "I've been so worried!"

Back at home in the lighthouse and tucked up warmly in his bed, Henry thought of Baby Seal safely at home with her mother. He had no trouble sleeping that night... no trouble at all.

The Polar Bear Paddle

Alfie the polar bear **loved** water more than anything else in the world.

He loved water so much that he could happily spend all day floating quietly like a humpback whale, with the fishes swimming around him.

He could dive and make huge splashes
in the water, and tumble like a
blurry snowball.

And he could swim, too.
But he only ever swam in the baby pool.

31

Alfie couldn't swim like grown-up polar bears.
He could only do **the Polar Bear Paddle**.

Alfie's older brothers laughed at him.
"You're far too big for the baby pool," they said. "Why don't you swim in the sea like us?"

"But I don't know how," said Alfie. "Will you show me?"

"No, we're too busy for that!" said Alfie's brothers. "You'll have to teach yourself!" And they swam away together.

One day, Alfie was watching Diving Bird diving in the sea. He was ever so good at diving — much better than Alfie!

Plop!

"Maybe if I asked Diving Bird," Alfie thought, "he would help me swim in the sea like my brothers."

So Alfie asked Diving Bird, "How do you swim in the sea?"

"It's easy! Just flap your wings and pretend you are flying."

"But I haven't **got** wings!" said Alfie.

Suddenly, something went whizzing past.

WOOSH!

"What was that?"
asked Alfie.

"That was Seal.
She swims so well
that she thinks
she's a fish!"

"If only I could swim like a fish," thought
Alfie, "then I could swim in the sea like my
brothers! Maybe I'll ask Seal to help me."

Alfie climbed the steps to the top of Seal's slippery slide.

"I want to swim as well as you!" said Alfie. "How do you swim in the sea?"

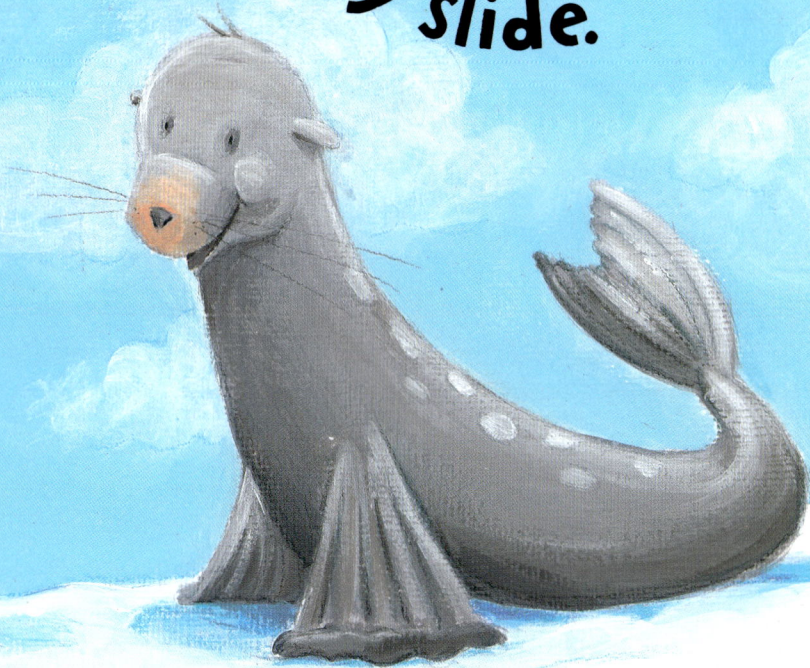

"I wriggle and squiggle!"

Alfie tried wriggling just like Seal, but he felt silly, and he didn't see how it would make him swim any better.

"That's it, Alfie!" called Seal.
"Keep SQUiggling!
Soon you'll be swimming
just like me!"

But Alfie went **faster** and **faster.** Seal's slippery slide was **SO** slippery that he couldn't stop!

And when he reached the bottom of the slide...

39

Alfie flew through the air and kept on going! He was very frightened, but there was nothing he could do to stop himself.

"That's it, Alfie!" called Diving Bird. "Flap your wings and close your eyes."

"My eyes are already closed!" shouted Alfie.

"And I can't flap my wings, because I don't have any!"

And the next moment...

41

SPLOSH!

Alfie landed in the sea with a mighty splash!
He tried wriggling and squiggling like Seal.
He flapped his arms like Diving Bird.

But it still didn't work.
And, in the end, Alfie just
did the Polar Bear Paddle.

When Alfie opened his eyes, he saw
everyone clapping and waving!

"You were brilliant, Alfie!" shouted
his brothers. "Will you show us how
you dive in? Please, Alfie."
"Okay," said Alfie. "I will!"

Alfie took his brothers to the top of
Seal's slippery slide.
     "Ready?" he asked.

Alfie's brothers wobbled
about on the ice, and looked
down at the sea below.
"Yes, we think so," they said,
trying to sound brave, but
feeling scared.

44

"Then **GO!**" shouted Alfie, and his brothers dived down the slide.

They **wriggled** and **squiggled** down like Seal...

"**wHEEEEE!**" they called as they slid down, down, down, until finally...

45

They zipped off the end of the slide and flew through the air, flapping their arms like Diving Bird.

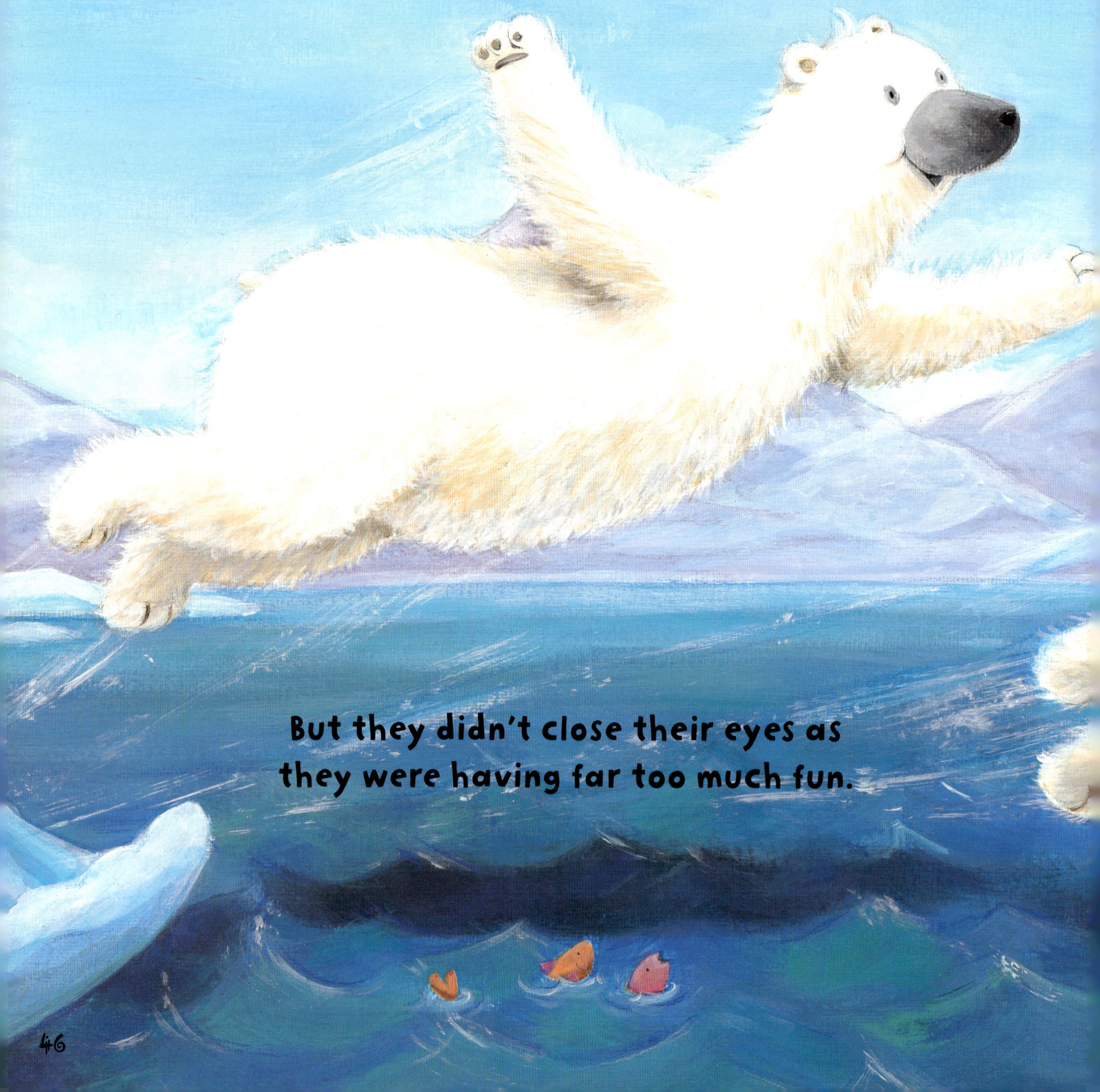

But they didn't close their eyes as they were having far too much fun.

"YIPPEee!"

And then...

they dived into the sea, making the biggest splashes Alfie had ever seen. Diving Bird cheered loudly.

SPLASH!

SPLOSH!

49

After that, Alfie didn't have to swim in the baby pool any more. He could swim in the sea with his brothers.

He didn't have to flap his arms like Diving Bird or wiggle and squiggle like Seal. He was perfectly happy swimming like a polar bear.

"It's called the Polar Bear Paddle!"
Alfie told his brothers.
And he soon showed everyone
else how to do it, too!

That's the One!

It was Friday, and Billy's mum and dad had an invitation to a party. But the invitation had been held up in the post, and the party was the next night. So soon!

"I fancy something different to wear," said Billy's mum. "A new look!"
"Sorry, but I can't help you choose," Billy's dad said. "I've got to go to work."
Billy's eyes lit up.

I'll come! I'll help you choose – and I can spend my birthday money from Nan.

Good idea!

said Dad.

Billy's dad worked at **Fast-Fix.**

Billy liked to sit in the office and watch his dad at work. But today, Billy had a job to do, too.

Mum drove them into town. Try It On was the best place to look for Mum's new clothes. "Something different," she said.

Try It On

OPEN

Jack and Jill's

First, Mum chose a pretty blouse and a leather skirt with tassels. She showed them to the shop assistant, went into the changing rooms – and out came a cowgirl, like in a Western film!

"That's the one!" said Billy. And it gave him an idea. He could choose a cowboy hat as his birthday present.

"I look like I've lost my horse," Mum said, shaking her head.

Next, she picked a short dress in black-and-white stripes.

She showed it to the shop assistant, went into the changing rooms – and out came a sporty girl footballer, like in the women's team in the park.

"That's the one!" said Billy.
And it gave him a different idea.
He could choose a football for himself.

But Mum shook her head.
"That's not a winner!"

Then she chose a long,
bright dress with a pattern
of exotic flowers. She
showed it to the shop
assistant, went into the
changing rooms – and out
came a girl from Jamaica.

"That's the one!" said Billy.
And it gave him another idea.

He could choose a steel drum as his present.

"It doesn't bang the drum for me," Mum said. Now she chose a white silk blouse and matching headscarf.

She showed them to the shop assistant, in she went – and out came a pirate, as exciting as Captain Annie in Billy's *Sea Fighters* book.

"That's the one!" said Billy. And what about a pirate's telescope for himself?

"Doesn't grab me," Mum said.
Her final choice was a pretty green
top with a wide, white collar and
matching tights. She showed them to
the shop assistant, in she went for
the last time – and out came
Robin Hood from the pantomime.

"That's the one!" said Billy.
Great – a bow and arrow for a present!

"Misses the target with me," Mum sighed.
So, they went to Jack and Jill's to choose Billy's present.

Mum was disappointed that she hadn't found anything to wear, but Billy looked high and low until he saw just the thing –

a little red sports car.

"That's the one!" Billy said. "For sure."

Drive with care

Dad came in wearing his dirty dungarees.

How did you get on? Dad asked.

But suddenly,
Mum was giving Dad
a long, hard look.

Wait and see!

Billy frowned.
He didn't get it.
Not at all.

It was the party night and Dad was waiting to go.

Are you ready yet? We're going to be late!

he called up the stairs.

"Nearly ready!"
Mum shouted back.

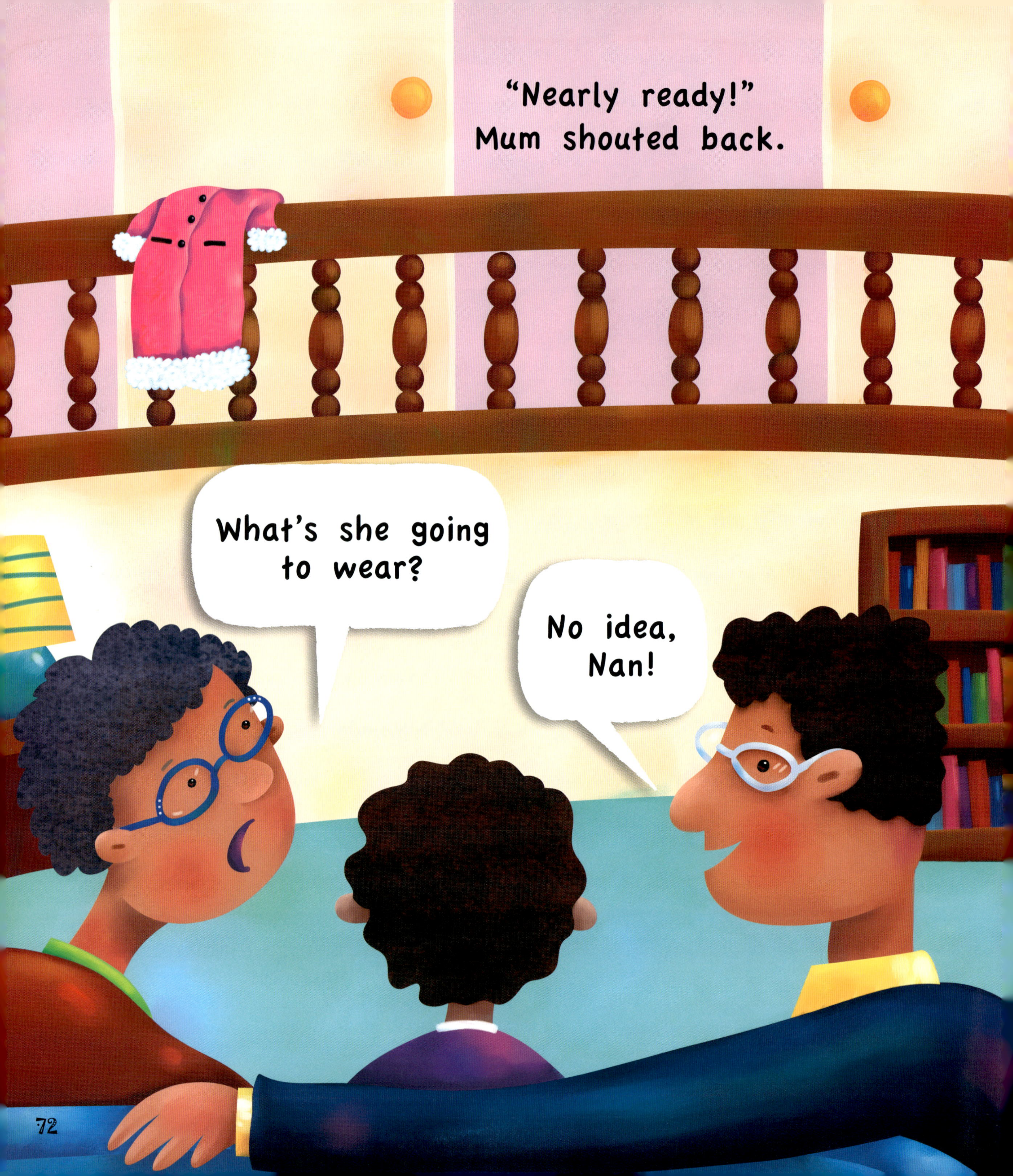

They heard the bedroom door open. Mum was coming! And she looked lovely.

Her necklace and her earrings sparkled, and so did her shiny, red shoes.

She couldn't have chosen anything more beautiful to wear than Dad's clean dungarees.

"That's the one!" said Billy and Dad together.

Albert
and
Sarah Jane

Albert and Sarah Jane were the very best of buddies. Their favourite thing was to curl up in a great big cat-dog cuddle by the fire every night, where it was safe and warm.

But there was one thing Albert
liked even better than that.

And that was eating his yummy
scrummy crunchies, from his big blue bowl.

And there was one thing he liked even better than **that**. And that was eating Sarah Jane's even yummier scrummier fishy nibbles.

He'd pinch one or two from her little red bowl, when his buddy wasn't looking, and they always tasted so much better than his own.

But one morning, while Sarah Jane was out and about early, Albert got a bit carried away with his nibbling.

mmmmmmm

So that when his pal came back in from the garden, very hungry and looking forward to her breakfast, she found there wasn't a speck of food left in her little red bowl.

And when she looked to see if there was
anything in Albert's big blue bowl...

she found there wasn't
a speck of food there, either!

Feeling confused, she went to find Albert and ask him why they hadn't any food to eat, but Albert was fast asleep in his basket.

That's odd, she thought, I'm sure he's fatter than usual. And I'm sure he smells all fishy, too!

"You've been eating my food, you naughty dog!" hissed Sarah Jane, arching her back.

But Albert kept his eyes closed. He snored away and ignored her.

83

There was nothing Sarah Jane could do to wake up Albert.

"Right," she said. "I've had enough of this!" And she turned round and marched straight out of the house.

Albert opened one eye, and
saw her going out of the cat flap.

She'll be back, he thought.
She always comes back.

But Sarah Jane didn't come back. If her owners wouldn't feed her and Albert was too tired to listen to her, she would go elsewhere. She wandered over to next door and decided to live there, instead.

By evening, Albert was lonely. By morning, he was howling at the cat flap.

"Come home, Sarah Jane!" he cried.

I miss you!

Albert spotted Sarah Jane through the upstairs window, looking happy and cosy.

He smiled at her, in a doggy sort of way, hoping to get her attention, but Sarah Jane ignored him.

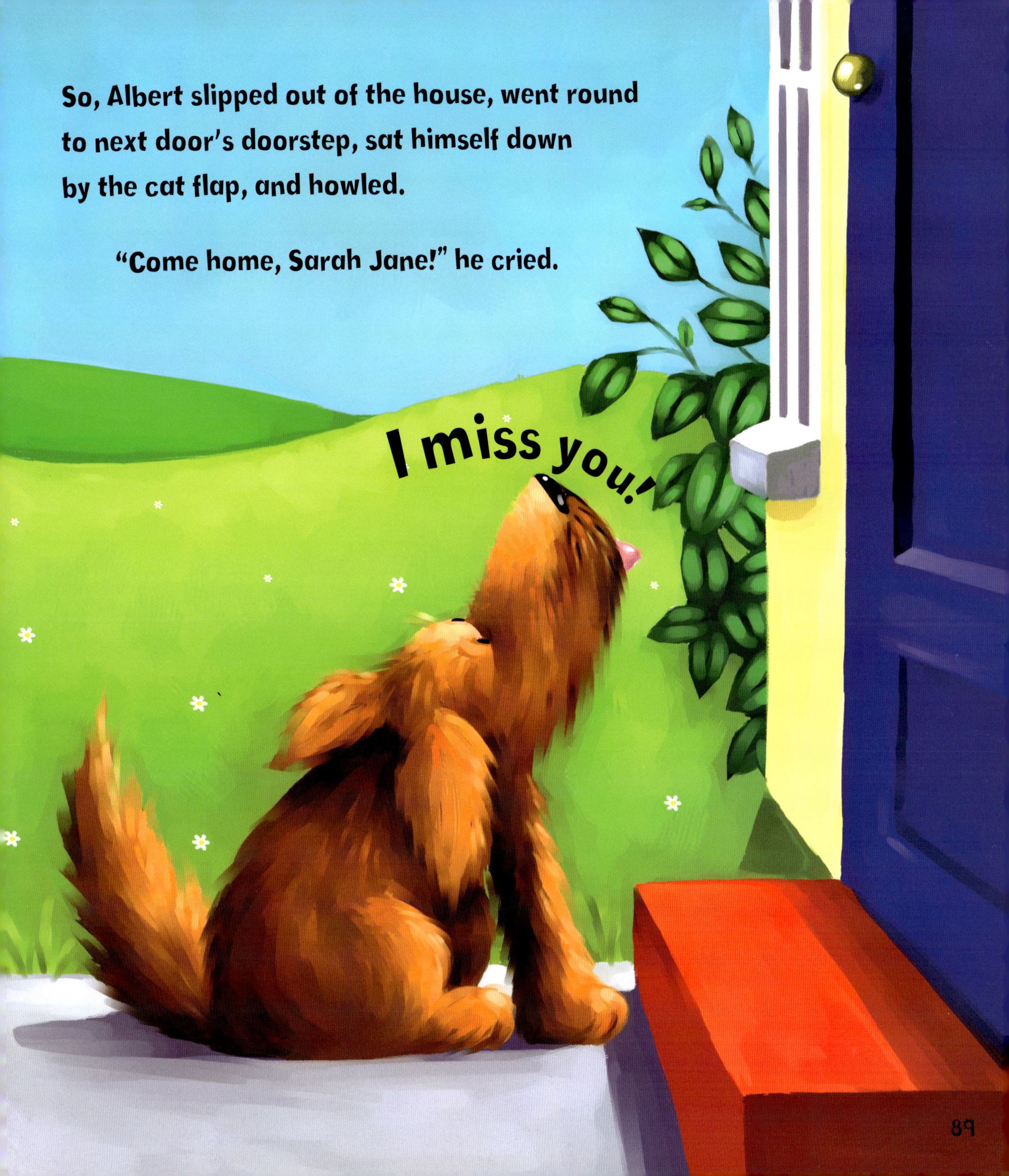

So, Albert slipped out of the house, went round to next door's doorstep, sat himself down by the cat flap, and howled.

"Come home, Sarah Jane!" he cried.

I miss you!

Soon Sarah Jane came down to see what all the fuss was about.
"Be quiet and stop howling, you naughty dog!"
hissed Sarah Jane, when she saw that it was Albert.

"But I'm sad and lonely," said Albert.
"I want a great big cat-dog cuddle by the fire."

"Well, the food's better over here, and nobody steals it," said Sarah Jane, licking her paws.

"But I'll admit it's lonely here, too, without a big smelly lump of a dog to snuggle up to..."

"Do you mean me?" said Albert.

"Yes, you," said Sarah Jane.

"Do you miss me, too?" asked Albert.

"I do," said Sarah Jane.

"Well... I'm sorry," said Albert.

"What for?" asked Sarah Jane.

"For gobbling up all your fishy nibbles," said Albert. "They just taste so yummy!"

"But will you do it again?" asked Sarah Jane.

"I won't," said Albert. "I promise."

"Will you even nibble them?" asked Sarah Jane.

"I won't," said Albert.

"Good," said Sarah Jane.

So she marched back
into her very own house.
And Albert marched
in behind her. Sarah
Jane had a little nibble
from her little red bowl
and Albert had a big
nibble from his
big blue bowl...

And then they curled up together, in a great big
cat-dog cuddle by the fire, and fell asleep.

Notes for parents and teachers

The Littlest Lighthouse Keeper to the Rescue

- Henry lives in a lighthouse. Do the children know what a lighthouse is? Explain what lighthouses do and where they are built. Have any of the children seen a lighthouse?

- Henry and Puffin meet a whale, a dolphin and a turtle in the sea. Can the children think of other creatures that live in the water?

- Henry and Puffin are good friends and like helping anyone in trouble. Can the children think of a time when they helped someone? What did they do and how did they feel?

The Polar Bear Paddle

- Read the story to the children, then ask them to read it to you, helping them with unfamiliar words and praising them for their efforts.

- Alfie was scared to go out of his baby pool. Do the children think he was brave to go swimming in the sea? Discuss with them what it means to be brave.

- Ask the children to draw pictures of Alfie and the other characters in the story, using the illustrations in the book to help them. Use paints, crayons or coloured pencils to make them more colourful.

That's the One!

- Provide a dressing-up box for imaginative play. The children can act out the different characters in the story – for example, a football player or a pirate.

- Children are surrounded by words that can be useful in reading. How many words around them can the children read?

- Play can lead to stories. Note down the children's stories, then write them down in a special book for sharing. The children could illustrate the stories themselves.

Albert and Sarah Jane

- Ask the children to think of six dog's names and six cat's names and write them down.

- Ask the children if they think Sarah Jane was right to go and live next door.

- Ask the children if they have ever had a falling out with a friend. What happened and how did they feel? Did they apologize and become friends again?

- Ask the children if they think Albert had changed by the end of the story. If so, why and how did he change?